CHASING BUTTERFLIES AT MOONRISE

A COLLECTION OF POEMS

NEHA KIRPALANI

Made with ♥ on the Notion Press Platform
www.notionpress.com

Contents

Contents

Contents

Preface

"In your light I learn how to love. In your
beauty, how to make poems.
You dance inside my chest where no-one sees you,
but sometimes I do, and that sight becomes this art."

— Rumi

Contents

Contributors

Tea Luck Publishers

Edited by Paula Shene/ Hardeep Kaur

Layout by Tilak Dhiman

Cover picture by Joann Joseph

Cover Design by Joann Joseph

Tea Luck Publishers

For more information,

email - tealuckpublishers@gmail.com

www.tealuckpublishing.com

Acknowledgements

Someone wise once said to me: writing is one of the most naked forms of vulnerability. When a writer puts herself out there, she's in a trust fall with the reader – with the hope and expectation that her words will be received with kindness and understanding.

'Chasing Butterflies at Moonrise' is that trust fall for me.And while writing is a solitary act, the creation of this book certainly didn't occur in a vacuum. And so I have quite a few people to thank:

Firstly and forever, my mother – my biggest champion, my greatest cheerleader. Thank you for giving me wings and allowing me to attempt flight. For encouraging me to follow my path, for teaching me how to be unshakeably resilient in the face of life's miseries, for your humour and kindness and above all, for your unconditional love. Thanks for being the Lorelai Gilmore to my Rory. I am, because you are.

To my best friend, my anam cara, my other half: thank you for showing up in this existence. It's your arrival that's allowed me to show up on the page, day after day, even when it got impossibly difficult to just exist. The stars have recombined and aligned perfectly after many millennia to bring us together, and I am eternally grateful.

To my Dad and my incredible Dadi – thank you; I am grateful to

ACKNOWLEDGEMENTS

be descended from you. I can only strive to embody the strength, courage, kindness, and sheer life force of my rockstar Dadi.

I have endless gratitude to my friends and family, without whom I might not have got through the last two years. Thank you, a million times over. I deeply appreciate your constant friendship, endless love, and miraculous support. My fiercest little tribe: Tanya, Akanksha, Piyush, Sarah, Subhag, Varsha, Aditi, Priya, Tatiana, Nicole, Pari, Supriya – and countless others at various seasons in every new phase of life. To my LinkedIn Creator Accelerator tribe: I couldn't have done it, and continue to do it, without you!

To all the people I've loved before: our journey may not have been easy, but it made me who I am today. Your presence in my life has inspired my art.

My deepest gratitude to all the greats who came before me. I stand both in awe and on the shoulders of these giants, whose works have inspired me, made me cry, laugh, and believe in love (even when I didn't particularly want to). *Salut* to these masters at their craft: Salman Rushdie, Ernest Hemingway, Jalāl ad-Dīn Mohammad Rūmī, Maya Angelou, Pablo Neruda, Rainer Maria Rilke, Gregory David Roberts, Neil Gaiman, Hafez, Rupi Kaur, Lang Leav, Franz Kafka, Amanda Gorman, JK Rowling, Haruki Murakami, Rabindranath Tagore.

I'm constantly in awe of all the women who've fought (and are continuing to fight) the good fight. Thank you for inspiring me to be a better feminist: Simone de Beauvoir, Frida Kahlo, Betty Friedan, Ruth Bader Ginsburg, Deborah Frances-White, Phoebe Waller-Bridge, Malala Yousafzai, Oprah, Chimamanda Ngozi

Adichie, Emma Watson, Michelle Obama, Meghan Markle, and countless other women and men around the world.

A special thank you to Hardeep Kaur, Marketing Director, and Paula Shene, MD at Tea Luck Publishers. I'm grateful for your welcome into the literary world with this first book. Thank you, also, to Joann Joseph, for the cover illustration and design: you've truly brought my vision to life.

And finally, to you – the reader, who picked up this book when there are literally millions of others vying for your coveted attention – my thanks will never be enough. If this book made you smile, if it made you gasp, if it made you reminisce or relate in any way, I believe I've managed to repay my debt of gratitude. This one's for you. Stick with me, I promise I'm only getting started…

To me, writing isn't always words on a page. More often than not, it's the vivid imagery that goes on inside my head; the words that seem to stream from a typewriter deep within my soul to accompany that silent motion picture inside my mind's eye. I've been lucky enough to capture what happens inside and put pen to paper (or fingers to keyboard), and I hope I've been able transplant that soul song into other people's minds.

My final note of gratitude is for the universe: when I asked for the key to unlock the riches stored inside my soul, the universe simply handed me a pen.

1. SECTION1

STARDROPS & RAINLIGHT

2. Butterfly Kisses, Starlight Symphonies

I'd been struggling emotionally;
Suffocating.
And then you came along.
You're oxygen to a dying person.
We look at each other, and the relentless march of time ceases
Allowing us to spend hours
Just looking at each other, often not even touching.
Then, we begin
By tracing our fingers down the beloved's face
It feels like a map being read by a blind man
A map he's known intimately all his life, but forgotten.
Kisses on the cheek are followed by gentle, tender kisses.
You taste like honey, like liquid ambrosia:
Like amrit, my manna from heaven.
Your breath catches in my throat; my life comes sharply into
focus.
Every dream I've ever dreamt
Every wish I've ever made upon a star
Everything comes alive in vibrant technicolour.
(We are so filmy, after all).

When we're together, it's nothing short of magic.
The outside world ceases to exist.
All there is, is us, in the moment, loving each other, holding each
other.
It's beyond beautiful.
That first sight of you, and my foolish heart began to feel hopeful
again.
Butterflies chased each other in my stomach.
Yellow and red, we wore: stop and slow down.
Was that a sign from the universe?
One we are in no way paying heed to, though.

3. Stardust Memories

We're made of stardust,
You and I.
Years and years ago
When a star expanded
Streaking across the night sky
There was you
There was me
Bound together
Breathing the same molten heat.
So tightly wound, no one could say with any certainty
This was you
This was me.
Then the star exploded
Fragments shot through the atmosphere
We were rent apart
Whistling, shrieking, howling
From the agony of separation.
On one side of the earth, what formed was you
On the other end, there came to be me.
Today, when we meet
It feels like stars recombining
Like this was meant to be

There is no you
There is no me
There is only we.

• 5 •

4. Starlight

You're starlight under my skin
Woven into the very fabric of me.
From the minute we met
What could have stopped the oceans from rushing in?
These words seem futile
For our bodies write (writhe) in a different tongue.
Look, I am learning the language of you:
Your rounded vowels, angular consonants
I want to be your constant.
Every arch of your back: a heart attack
My heart skips more than a beat.
Your skin: its searing heat
There's nowhere else I'd rather be
Than tucked away in your arms
My face buried in the crook of your neck.
Skin upon skin upon skin
You bring me back from the edge of the abyss
What magic is this?
This is how I feel you; this how I learn you
My body simply remembering your soul
Like meeting an old friend, an anam cara
Across time, across space

Separated by many millennia
Fate's been kind enough to lead me back to you.

5. The Oasis

The traveller had been scouring the desert in a mad, frenzied
search for water
Days and weeks had gone by with nothing to quench their thirst
Then, as night fell, just as suddenly the clouds parted
And the moonlight shone on an oasis.
Is this a mirage? they wondered.
Anxious yet eager, they crawled on their hands and knees
Towards this shimmering light of promised salvation.
And when they got there, their eyes couldn't believe the sight they
witnessed:
A golden lagoon filled with liquid light
Date palms, fragrant flowers: a veritable paradise
And best still, water enough to last seven lifetimes!
The moon, a cold compress on a fevered night.
The stars, distant yet near, casting their pale light.
The waves unfurling underfoot like bales of undulating silk.
This is what it feels like, to have found you and made you mine.

6. An Entanglement of Limbs

Arms intertwined
Your legs on mine
We sleep, afraid of separation.
In our dreams, making a reparation.
I breathe out, you breathe in
Warm breath intermingles.
This ain't no sin
I love it when your nose crinkles.
Your dreams seem hopeful,
You sigh a little sigh
You make me humble
To you, I'd never lie.
Our destinies intertwined
Your heart in mine
We live, hoping for salvation
With our love, making a salutation:
To all that is good and pure
To all we hold true and dear.
This entanglement of limbs
This entanglement of lives.

7. Whiskey-Laced Whispers

How to extricate myself from your arms?
You look at me
My soul catches fire
And like a phoenix, I rise from the ashes
Of all old loves.
Under your gaze, I am born anew.

8. Apocalypse

Everything the light touches is ours.
Every breath. Every kiss. Every heartbeat.
Isn't it all bathed in the light of our love?
The sound of your laughter, a gurgling river
Created just to quench my thirst.
You are my everything.
Never has been, never will be
Anyone as perfect as you
Your lips my lips
Apocalypse.
You bring me back to myself
You make me more myself
The things I'd forgotten
The love I'd saved inside me
With no one to give to
It's all pouring out now
Raining down on you
Are you drenched yet?

9. Apocalypse II

I trace your lips with my fingertips.
I trace them with my lips.
Can't you see?
It's like the apocalypse.
The moonlight
The stars
You've given me everything:
My shining star.
When I'm with you I want for nothing
You bring me back to life
You bring me back to love.
You are love. It's been you all along
I'm glad we took a chance on each other;
Look what we might have missed.
You make me believe
You make me live in the now
You've taught me to appreciate this moment
For its universe of possibilities
For its blessings
It's true: we've been blessed.
You make me want to be better
We are good for each other

We are good to each other
This is how it's supposed to be.

10. On the River of Dreams

There's a river in our bedroom
The bed: our life raft.
Watch these waves unfurl
Watch time wash over us
It's a benediction.
Clouds of silk
Candy skies
The sun, our fireball
The moon, our dreams made real
The stars come out at night
Just to say hi
Winking, twinkling
Shining in a crimson sky.
Every minute with you is magic.
Every minute. Every breath. Every kiss.

11. Noir Daydreams

Hunger:

Use time and space to your advantage
Tear two people apart
And watch them burn
As hunger licks their insides.
Their ache? It's palpable.

Thirst:

Make a wish
Make a desperate plea
Supplicate all the heavenly Gods
Pray in fevered desire.
The rains? They're coming, sure as hell.

Dreams:

Take your hand
And place it upon the other's
Lay skin upon skin upon skin.
Make way for lingering kisses, invisible, unseen
Recognised them yet for what they are?
Faint traces of a long-forgotten dream.

12. Moonrise Queendom

The moon is our traveling troubadour
Visiting our window every night
Begging for an audience
Waiting patiently for us to turn to her
Singing her lament when we don't
Beaming with joy when we do.
The moon wants nothing from us
Nothing but our togetherness
That's the currency she'd like to be paid in
That's the price of her performance.
And perform she does, for us:
Every night
Night after night
Changing costumes, shape shifting,
In and out of form.
All in an attempt to steal our attention
To entice us to look away from each other
For just one second
So we'd notice the magnificence of her beauty.
I'm oblivious to her charms.
I see nothing,
Until my chand ka tukda looks up, moonward.

In your eyes I see the whole universe
Galaxies grow bigger as your pupils expand
The Milky Way shrinks to a dot when they contract
The whole world melts away
I see only you.

13. A Pocketful of Starlight

We are up in the mountains
There's no one here but you and me.
I bring a book;
You laugh and ask me cheekily
If reading is all I intend to do
While I'm here with you.
I smile
Mark my place in the book
Flip it over
And lean in for a kiss.
I can feel your skin as it rearranges into a smile
I can hear your dimples flicker on.
I kiss your smile
And the night sky instantly lights up in stars.
Purple meets streaks of light
This is everyday magic.

14. What I Like

What I like:
Reading in bed
Watching in my mind's eye
As the prince slays the evil dragons
In his quest to rescue the beautiful princess.
The first bite of a piping hot slice of pizza,
When the cheese burns a hole in the roof of my mouth.
A hot shower
The rivulets of soothing water running down my skin,
Washing away the scourge of the day.
What I love:
You.

15. Everywhere

Ratatat tat

Ratatat tat tat

Ratatatatatatatat

My mind's whirring

The pace keeps increasing

Like a washing machine on full spin.

Your hands your hands your hands

On my skin

When did you grow a third hand?

Feels like you have a hundred hands

They're clawing my skin, touching me

Everywhere everywhere everywhere

My mind is so aware

My body is so aware

Tingling with goose bumps:

Each pore in attendance

Standing straight in

A t t e n t i o n.

Skin meets skin meets skin

There is no definitive answer

For where I end and you begin

It's nuclear fusion

Or is it nuclear fission?
Which is the hotter one?
How is it that I'm both primal and
S u b l i m a l?
Both frenzied and zen-like?
When your hands your hands your hands.
Paint a symphony
On the blank canvas of my skin?
When they write an aria worthy of Liszt
A sonata befitting Schubert
A hundred orchestras
A thousand crescendos.
Birds fly
Everywhere everywhere everywhere
And I'm so aware
I'm so blissfully aware.
I'm so fully here
In this moment
In this passionate embrace
As your hands travel
Everywhere everywhere everywhere

16. SECTION 2

MOSAIC-TINTED MEMORIES

17. One Word Love Story

18. The Glasshouse

People who live in glass houses shouldn't throw stones, they say.
But what if you're only visiting one? What rules apply then?
Not that we were there to pelt stones at one another.
In fact, dinner that night
Almost half a decade ago
Felt like the exact opposite of hatred: it felt like love.
I can't remember whose birthday it was
And I guess it doesn't even matter.
There was cake.
You ordered us a chicken teriyaki pizza,
Fish & chips,
And a bottle of red.
I could see you were in a mood to celebrate.
This was the freest I'd seen you in months;
It felt like you'd let finally your guard down, for just one
moment.
I actually believed that night you'd finally let me in.
I watched as the wine worked its way through your bloodstream
Every subsequent glass enlarging and reddening your cheeks.
We laughed, we spoke, we drank.
Like I said, it felt like love.

You spoke to me about your dreams for the future
Dreams I realised would never include me
Dreams I still fervently and silently prayed you'd achieve.
I told you about my fears.
You listened, smiled, held my hand and told me things would get
better.
They did, but you weren't around to see it.
You weren't around to watch me conquer my demons.
I slayed those dragons all on my own and turned around,
Triumphant, half expecting you to be standing there
With that blazing look of pride and love in your eyes.
You weren't.
A lot has changed since that night.
We no longer speak.
You probably no longer even think of me.
I almost never think of you.
Life happened, and it took us a lifetime to get here.
Where is here?
For me, here is my childhood home, my bedroom, my life.
Like time stood still, even though the world has flipped 180.
For you, here is a world so far removed from that glasshouse
That the latter may not even seem real anymore.
I guess it's a testament to how much things have changed
That our glasshouse no longer exists.
In its stead stands a formulaic coffee house.
Go figure.
People in glasshouses shouldn't throw stones.

I never really did apologise for that other night, did I?
It was your birthday
(Another year older, another year unwiser, another year fiercely
loved by yours truly).
I'm sorry I ruined your night,
I'm sorry I screamed and raved and ranted for what seemed like
hours,
I'm most sorry you made me cry, also for hours.
We argued:
You threw some heavy metaphorical stones, and so did I.
Looking back, maybe mine never hit their mark
Maybe you had just immunised yourself against the vitriol.
Yours, on the other hand, have left some pretty indelible scars.
Like they say, people in glasshouses …
And speaking of birthdays, we made a pact for a milestone
birthday.
Naïve me, I actually thought you'd hold up your end of the deal.
Come October 4th, I half expected my doorbell to ring
And for you to come bounding in through the door,
Like you had countless times before.
I guess I've been subconsciously pushing everyone away
Sabotaging every relationship over the years,
In the desperate hope you'd honour our pact.
I dreamt of that happening for months before my birthday.
In the waking world, the doorbell stayed silent.
My phone screen never lit up with your name flashing on it.
You carried on as if we'd never promised each other the world.

I guess only I did.

19. Lucky In Love

People say writers are the luckiest in love
They're the only ones who win
Whether Love stays or leaves.
For when Love leaves, a writer turns the pain into art.

20. Half-Remembered Dream

You come to me
Like a half-remembered dream.
Your face swims
In and out of focus.
I clutch at the image,
Like a child clutches at straws.
And then the morning comes
Turning you into smoke.
You are the half-remembered dream
The one I'll never be able to never forget.

21. When Will We Collide?

22. A Parallel Reality

23. Time

Time: it can do some pretty devastating things.
A year goes by,
And you find yourself
At the edge of a precipice
Looking down
Dizzily into the abyss
Willing yourself not to fall.
A year ago,
You held your lover in your arms.
You could see him
Clear as the light of day.
Now, he sits across from you
Already a million miles away.
Time: it can do some pretty shattering things.
They say Time heals,
That all a broken heart needs
Is some space to breathe.
And there will come a time,
As sure as today will become yesterday,
Tomorrow becomes today,
When you'll be back in the beloved's arms
As if the intervening Time

Never happened at all.

24. Loneliness

What of loneliness?
It makes us do things;
Hold on to broken people
Longer than we should.
So that our own jagged edges
Combine noiselessly with theirs
Piercing skin, drawing forth crimson blood.
We don't mean to hurt each other
And yet we do;
We are merciless.
Let us blame our aloneness
For it makes us do these terrible things.

25. The Lover's Pilgrimage

A visit to the city you once lived in
Would have meant walking in your footsteps.
It would have involved
Seeing what you once saw,
Breathing the anointed air you once took in,
My feet kissing the cobbled streets
You once walked in.
But now you've been long gone.
Visiting your city would have been a lover's pilgrimage
But one I was never able to make.

26. The Whole Picture

What I believed to be light
Has befuddled me.
Turned into the murkiest, stickiest darkness;
The type where you can't even see your hands
Even when you hold them up right in front of your face.
I can't trust my senses anymore
I don't know which way is up.
"The only people who see the whole picture
Are the ones who step out of the frame"
But what happens if the canvas has ripped,
And the picture has left the frame;
What, then?

27. The Broken Pieces of my Heart

You walk away from me
Back turned; and step into the ocean
Ready to disappear into the waves
As if nothing happened
As if the intervening months have meant nothing;
Nothing at all, less than nothing.
As if they've been my delusion
A figment of my overactive imagination.
You walk into the waves
But what of the devastation you've left in your wake?
Who will pick up the pieces
Of my broken heart?

28. Bad Habit

I am beginning to feel the first pangs of separation from you
Knowing fully well that it was me
Who vehemently insisted on us being apart;
At least for a few days.
You called and spoke with me before my eyes even opened this
morning
And it felt like love.
Even this fight, this uljhan, this pain feels like love.
Everything about us feels like love.
We don't need to label what we have but it's certainly some form
of love.
Far beyond friendship but a little less than lovers.
Our bodies may never intertwine
But our souls have been in union before time
Look, they're in union right now.
I know you are thinking of me as I write these words
You are trying to make sense of our hijr, our moment of
separation
Trying to make sense of what it is you feel for me
And how this feeling confuses everything you know and hold true
about yourself.

*I hear the azaan now – it's been weeks since I heard this
beautiful sound
And it seems like a sign that everything will be alright.
That my heartbreak and pain and loneliness are not for nothing.
That there is a divine plan and it shall be revealed in due course
Because we are meant for bigger things.
I miss you. I miss us, whatever we were.
2020 has been a bizzarre trip,
So it's no surprise your arrival and departure
Fit the theme of this crazy year too.
On the plus side of all this, you're fuelling my writing so that's
something, eh?
Let's call it: the diamond in the shitshow.
But seriously, who even begins an apology with "I'm sorry if…"?
A person who can't accept responsibility
For the hurt and pain they cause in their wake.
In other words, a tornado of a person.
What we forgive in those we don't care for
We can't tolerate in the ones we truly love.
Every instinct in me is screaming I let go
While every nerve and fibre of my being is craving to hold on.
What is this yearning?
What to speak of this pining?
Who are we to each other and why are we not able to recognise
it?
We are each other's bad habit.*

29. The Anatomy of Anger

Calm down.

Take a deep breath.

Stem that flow of adrenaline coursing through your veins.

Yes, it's exhilarating

To feel like you've been wronged.

Yes, your body wants out

But you've got to just breathe:

Let it all out.

Hush that ringing in your head.

Honey, it's doing you no favours.

You are not your anger.

You are not the beast hungering for revenge.

You are the dove, majestic and powerful.

Take flight.

Loosen the chains that shackle you to the present.

It will not be easy.

Let me say that again: it will not be easy.

The red hot tongue of anger will lick your insides

Refusing to release you from its vice-like grip.

It will tunnel your vision.

It most certainly will constrict your chest.
The wolf of anxiety will prowl
On the edges of your consciousness
Waiting for a single moment of weakness
So she can slip through the gaps
And swoop in for the kill.
But unclench that fist.
Unmesh those teeth.
Widen those narrow slits the anger has forced your eyes to
become.
Bite back that harsh tirade.
Blink away the tears.
One breath.
And another.
And another.
This is how you defeat the monster.

30. This is Not a Love Letter

This is not a love letter.
I repeat: this is not a love letter.
This is a letter to Love
That devious miscreant
Who for years has kept us ensnared,
Tormented and beguiled.
It's charmed, seduced, and used every trick in the book
To keep us hooked.
That devil
Who has come and gone
Moved on
While ensuring we couldn't.
Dear Love,
This is the end of the road.
Sincerely,
The lovelorn.

31. Thank You

Thank you for existing
It's how I know pure goodness is alive.
Thank you for loving me
It's how I felt the grace of the divine.
Thank you for leaving me
It's how I learned to love myself.

32. SECTION 3

WHIPLASH

33. Solitary Confinement

When you force someone into solitary confinement
How can you wonder when they reach out to their neighbour in
the next cell?
How can you not assume they'd crave a connection?
Our minds can be the quietest, darkest place
Full of screaming horrors, ginger fears
Why wouldn't we want to find someone to share this mad world
with?

34. Time Outside of Time

I'm loving this time outside of time
This heady intoxication of you
You turn to look at me
And your gaze sears my soul.
The words I whisper to you
In the dead of the night
Are the only words left in this world
Where words have temporarily been suspended.
One more night, and there is no need for language
In this meeting of souls:
Our hearts understand each other perfectly.
Like two compatible puzzle pieces
It just fits. We just fit.
We are learning to fall in step
Learning, or should I say re-learning
Our unique dance, our little foxtrot.
Sometimes, I'll admit, we are misaligned
But that's only because
We are learning each other in this existence:
This physical presence.

For I'm certain we've met before
And in all of our past encounters
Across time and space, we've been exactly so:
Soulmates, anam caras, lovers, friends.
It matters not what form our love takes
We have always been in each other's orbit
Circling one another, magnetically aligned
Existing as a true union of souls
Pure energy and light.

35. A Lockdown Love Story

Swipe right
Swipe left
Swipe left
Yawn
Scratch scratch
Swipe right
Blink
Match.
Witty opening line
Crickets
Unmatch
The End.

36. Asking for a Friend

When time is standing still
Like it has been since 2020
How long will it take
For a departed love to fade
And become a distant memory?

37. Old Friends

Almost every time I wake up from sleep,
I find three of my old friends at my bedside.
Anxiety sits to my left
While Breathlessness and Constricted Chest
Are sat on the other side.
I recognise these companions as guardians from my past.
But today, the four of us had a little chat;
Well, I did most of the talking – for a change
I plucked up the courage and let them know
In no uncertain terms, that I've now outgrown their friendship.

38. Note to Self

Turn your attention inwards and allow space
For your emotions to breathe.
Let them roam your body freely
While you sit with them in silence
Simply bearing witness.
Don't deny them the right to do as they please
Make no mistake – these emotions are like spoilt children
They will create havoc if you so much as say
'Stop', or 'No', or 'Go to your room'.
Develop the wisdom and courage
Kindness and self-compassion
When dealing with your emotions.
They're valid – just as valid as you are
And they desperately need your attention.
It is their function to protect you.
And so you must thank them for their efforts
Be kind, but let them know you don't need their protection.
Simply say to them:
I'm okay for now.
Sit with your pain and heartbreak and loneliness and worry.
Hear them out patiently, kindly, and with all the attention you
can muster.

This is the only way to stop them from following you around all
day
Threatening to scream themselves hoarse to get you to listen.
Let them say their piece.
Once they have, thank them for trying to protect you.
And say this to them in return: I'm okay for now.
I'm okay for now.
I'm okay for now.

39. Return to Wholeness

Sit with the grief and the pain
And let each have its say.
Listen to your heart
And give yourself an abundance of love
As you would to a child whose favourite toy has broken.
Set aside things that don't serve you anymore.
The news that amplifies collective fear
Technology that keeps you up at night
The pressure to stay productive
(And broadcast it on social media).
Dial down the cacophony.
Let your quiet heart lead you back to wholeness.

40. Lockdown Lessons

It feels like the world's being picked apart – piece by piece
Only to be put together anew.

There is a paradise within, but equally an inferno.
Our days are spent doing a delicate dance between both.

Gratitude and despair
Faith and disbelief
Hope and surrender
It's no longer hard to hold
Two conflicting emotions at the same time, in the same breath.
The important question, really, is
Which of these to breathe in, and which of them to release?

And so you must treat yourself with extreme kindness;
Develop courageous compassion
And weaponised self-mercy.
Learn to self-soothe.
The only way out is through.

This is a mass return to origin.

Love is where we came from.
Love is where we're headed towards.

~

But my question is this:
Where is the PPE for the heart?
Where can I buy a hazmat suit to protect from catching feelings?

~

I guess what I'm trying to say is:
It's okay if your mind is a slippery slope at the edge of the
universe
It's okay for it to go to pieces sometimes.
What's important is to walk yourself down from that ledge
As often as you can and with as much determination
As if it were your closest friend.

~

Put your hand on your heart and say to yourself:
I live in a friendly universe
The universe is protecting me from harm.
Things are in motion in the universe
To bring me exactly what I need in this moment
I am opening myself up to the positive forces in the universe
And everything is now falling into place.
There is only love, light, and healing.

41. When the Apocalypse Comes

And when the apocalypse comes,
As it inevitably will one day,
Let them find you exactly as you are right now:
Strumming that guitar
Or wielding that paintbrush
Or writing your pain away.
In other words,
When the end of days arrives,
Let them find you doing what you love best.

42. SECTION 4

BUTTERFLIES RISING

43. Raindrops on a Windowsill

First came torrential love
Then came soul-wrenching pain
Then came the words
Quiet and unbidden, like the falling rain.
All I could really do was sit by
And watch, as they took form,
My job was simply to type them up, write them down
And try to make sense of it all.

44. Why I Write

Since I gave you my book of poetry
I now have no option but to write poetry myself
Every time I think of you.
I write because there are things I cannot — will not — say to you.
I tell the world how I feel because I can't tell you.

45. 193 Views

My IG stories have an average of
A hundred and ninety three views
And not a one from you.
Do you know the punchline of this joke?
You're the one I've been writing to.

46. Rain

I'm my own worst enemy.
I flood the ones I love
Drown them sometimes
In the sheer force of my being.
At other times, I leave them unquenched
The parched earth of their soul
Waiting for the shower of my love.
Either a drought or a thunderstorm.
Nothing in between.
I've never learned balance.
I'm my own worst enemy.
I am, rain.

47. The Muse has No Sense of Timing

Constantly at the beck and call of the muse
Who seems to have no concept of timing.
I waited for her all day yesterday
Cleared my schedule
And say at my desk
Hoping she'd show up.
She turned up at 2.30 last night
And forced me to write
Until the wee hours of the morning.
The result of that work
Is in front of you now.
This arrangement of words
They sometimes call a poem.

48. The Desert Rains

The muse's attention
Can be as fickle as the desert rains.
Far too often, the parched earth of the soul
Craves the shower of words
But when the rain comes
It is paradise.
This torrential downpour
Is magical.
It washes away the dirt from the soul
And has the power to heal
The most wretched of hearts.

49. Midwives

We aren't writing:
We are just bearing witness
To the words that come and go
Of their own accord.
All they're doing is
Using us as midwives
In an attempt to be born.

50. A Writer's Greatest Fear

There are a great many horrifying things in this world:
Monsters and demons
And spirits tearing up our lives
Like a child sometimes rips up his own playthings.
Then there's the pain of unrequited love.
But there's nothing scarier for a writer
Than when the ink runs dry
And the words fail to come.

51. The Warrior

She didn't choose to become
But was transformed
Into the warrior she now is.
The world made her shed her soft edges
And grow an exoskeleton
To contain the storm within
That was wrapped in skin.
She is a force of nature
Like the wind
She cannot be contained.
She is you. She is me. She is we.
Dedicated to all the women of steel.

52. Bang.

The gun went off
Shattering the eerie stillness
That was characteristic of pre-dawn.
"I must remember to pick up the laundry today."
"I can't believe he said that to me.
He's going to have to pay for that later."
"She shouldn't have worn that dress."
"I hope the kids will be alright."
Bang.
In the infinitesimal seconds it took
For the bullet to hit its target with a soft thud
A world of possibilities played out
Only to be cruelly exterminated in the end.
And all that was left in its wake
Were a few wisps rising from a still-smoking barrel.

53. The Storyteller

I pull a story out of thin air.
'Love', because really, what else is there?
'You', because you mean the world to me.
'I', because where you are, there I am.

54. Ink-Stain Tattoos

This is the mental image I cherish of myself:
Ink-stains crawling up my wrists to my elbows
Surrounded by sheafs of paper and my journals
Hair askew, horn-rimmed glasses,
A glass of wine in hand
Make that a whiskey –
I've always been a whiskey girl.
The late afternoon sun pouring through my French windows
While I listen to French jazz
Did I mention that I love French?
I used to dream in the language – once upon a time
But that time has long past
That was a different me
Very different from the one you now see
The one who writes and writes and writes
Through the day and all through the night.
It's like these words are screaming to be born
I'm just the medium, I take no credit for bringing them to life
They come to me from a higher place
And bid me to record dutifully everything they say
And so all I can do is write and write and write.

And that's why you'll find me
On any given Sunday
Tattooed with ink stains
Buried under mountains of paper
Dreaming up better lands
Feverishly wishing for better tomorrows
Willing them into existence
While I
Write and write and write.

55. SECTION 5

HEARTS AFLUTTER

56. Flighty Grains of Sand

I know you've had that moment too. When you look over at
someone and in that moment,
you feel a mutual sense of perfect understanding. It's like both of
your eyes light up and you
think to yourself "where have you been all this while?" and you
know, beyond a shadow of
doubt, that the other person feels the exact same way about you.
And this happens so imperceptibly and so often that it's easy not
to even notice it or pay it
any attention, but the truth is in that moment of perfect
understanding and realisation, what
passes between two souls — and I'm talking souls here, so it ain't
got nothing to do with
boyfriend/girlfriend, lover, husband, wife, significant other, none
of that rubbish but true
soul-connection — is love.
It's real and true and pure love and there's nothing more
exhilarating in the world.
And so we flit from moment to moment, day to day, lifetime to
lifetime looking for that true

connection, that soul-searing love, and that's why its pale imitation has us disappointed at best and downright depressed at worst.

It isn't because it's rare to find – it's ubiquitous – but because it's rare to hold.

Maintaining a connection like that is akin to holding flighty grains of sand in a closed palm.

57. Half Love

This is a story of hijr (separation) but equally of vasl (union).
This is the story of the boy who waltzed into my life with his Sufi
poetry and soulful eyes
like deep lagoons, Love stirring in them like a fantastic sea
creature.
For years, I watched him from afar as he travelled the country
with his performing troop of
Sufi musicians and storytellers, reviving the ancient art form of
dastangoi.
I was painfully shy at first; it took me two years to pluck up the
courage to even say hello and
tell him how much I adored his performances. At the rate our
dastan (story) was progressing,
it would have been another few years before we'd actually gone
out on a date.
Except fate had other plans for us.
A freak accident, a tragic loss of life, and the world of poetry will
never be the same again.
I still dream of this boy sometimes, the boy who could have been
my soulmate.
I still pray for this boy every night. My half love.

58. Chasing Butterflies

Once upon a time, there was a little girl who, on her daily walk,
stumbled upon a meadow.
She was drawn to the rustling of the wind as it grazed the
treetops. She took a tentative step,
afraid something would leap out at her from behind the trees.
When she assured herself it was
safe, she entered. It was only a few feet in before the grass tickled
her bare knees – scraped
and bruised from the last time she'd fallen. Which was mere days
ago. Yes, she was quite
accident-prone, it was true. But never mind that – let us return
to the little girl, who is now
looking up in wonder at the blue sky, watching the sun as it
plays hide-and-seek through a
blanket of snowy-white clouds – shining brightly one moment,
bathing the beautiful little girl
in sun; and just as quickly dipping behind the clouds and casting
long shadows across her
hopeful face.
She sits down, cross-legged, buried between the blades of grass. A
book magically appears at
her elbow. She picks it up. Takes one quick look at it and her

*heart leaps for joy: it is the
book she has been waiting for! The book of love, some call it. It's
leather-bound, heavy, and
she finds that it has a faint musty smell – it must be all those
years of being locked up in a
cold, dark bookcase that made it smell like this, she thinks to
herself. Just as she begins to
absorb herself amidst those honey-dew words, a butterfly flits
across her line of sight. In a
flash, she's on her feet. The book lays forgotten on the ground as
she tears after the butterfly,
delight shining in her face and bathing her every feature like
sweat. This was the moment
she'd been waiting for! The reason she'd entered the meadow on a
whim, even though she
didn't know it at the time. It's as if she had pre-arranged to meet
this very butterfly in this
very field, at precisely this moment in time.
She gives chase, eager to catch the butterfly. She wants to smell its
colours and hear its
fragrance. She wants to feel its soft wings as they beat gently in
the palm of her hand. In short, she want's to love it and be loved
by it.
But butterflies, they don't wait for little girls – they flit in and
out of sight like thoughts. They scramble, they hurry. Vamoose!
They're gone before you know it. They're known for their
flighty nature, for their inability to be captured and tamed. But*

see, our little girl is just as

quick – she runs like the wind, and doesn't like to be outpaced.

And oh! Miracle of miracles! She's caught it now – holding it

gently and firmly in an almost-closed fist that she holds above her

head, almost triumphantly. She has glee written all over her face.

As she loosens her grip – just a crack, to see how her new friend is

doing, see – the butterfly

seizes its opportunity and flies out of her hand. She gives chase,

but her heart isn't in it this

time. In a short while, she gives up, exhausted. She makes her

way back to her spot and

collapses into a dejected heap.

She spends an hour laid out like this, her back on ground, her

face turned towards the perfect

blue skies. It almost seems cruel; like the heaven above is

mocking her for failing. Even the

sun seems harsher in all its midday glory. She screws up her face

and closes her eyes – partly

to defend against the sun and also because she doesn't want to let

escape the single, lonely

tear that's begun to form at the corner of her right eye. Too late.

The tear slides down

anyway, lonely no more, for it is followed by another, and

another, and then another – until

she's sobbing furiously at the injustice of it all. She really had

wanted that butterfly with all

her heart; she'd yearned for it even before she knew what it was.

*And as she lay there, something wonderful happened. The rogue
butterfly returned, unbidden,
and landed softly on her upturned palm. It sat there tentatively,
and then spoke so softly that
she had to stop crying so she could listen to what it had to say.
Politely, as though someone
were knocking at an oak-panelled door in her grandfather's
study, it asked, "May I enter?"
Love had arrived. And this time, it intended to stay.*

59. Those Three Words

I must have arranged that combination of words any number of ways in conversation with

you. I must have said those three words any numbers of times when speaking with you.

"I" is a word that crops up so often, so interchangeably, when we talk. Is it even a singular

identity anymore between us? Have not our "I"s merged into a we?

"Love". Such a complicated word, such a simple emotion. Love is a many-splendoured thing

and all that, but cut away all the fluff; what's left is how it feels. How does it feel? Like your

heart is filled, overflowing, a balloon about to burst, a cup about to overflow. Centuries later,

with all the collective human knowledge and lived experience, we're no closer to

understanding what love is than we were in the caves. I think that's both a curse and a

benediction.

"You". What do I say about you? What hasn't been said, what can never be said, what should

always be said, prefixed to every zikr of you? Only that you are

everything. You live inside
me, everywhere, you're my everything: parent, offspring, mentor,
pupil, emperor, subject,
lover, friend. Friend. Like the one true Beloved – the one up
above. Does that explain why I
worship you? You said my love language was acts of service, isn't
love itself an act of
service? In praise of Love, I worship at the altar of you.
Arranged in the right combination, these three words mean
nothing-and-everything. Convey a
world of meaning but reveal nothing new. Haven't we always
known? Isn't this just us
remembering, reaffirming, reimagining, and revisiting what was
at once so obvious when we
first met? Was it when we first kissed, when we first held each
other, when I first drowned in
the deep lagoons of your eyes? Was it the fifth or tenth time? How
does it matter?
For someone whose life's purpose involves playing with words I'm
having a hard time telling
you how I feel. I'm struggling to say to you these three words;
they're said too much they're
not enough, Gary Lightbody was right.
But I know for a fact if I lay here, you'd lay with me and just
forget the world. We do this all
the time. We lose ourselves in ourselves. There is no me; there is
no you. There is only we.

About The Poet

Neha Kirpalani is also known as the warrior poet - softness and strength collide in her, much like waves crashing against a rock. Her love affair with words began at a young age; and writing has helped her face all of life's myriad challenges: adolescence, dating, heartbreak, separation, career transitions, adulting, and the pandemic circa 2020. Throughout her teenage years and early 20's, she's written numerous short stories, blogs, long-form articles and even a novel.

'Chasing Butterflies at Moonrise' is her first book of poetry, and deals with the themes of love, longing, loss, healing, and self-love. Born in Bombay, Neha studied in Bangalore, India and Manchester, United Kingdom. She began her career at Goldman Sachsas an investment banker, but later switched tracks to pursue her love for the written word. Since then, she's led a team ofcopywriters at a burgeoning creative agency, written for Bollywood, and currently works as a Senior Marketing Manager at a London-based company in the EdTech industry. In the past year, she's exercised her writing muscle, by contributing to the QS World University Rankings2022 Report and to Harvard Business Review.

Her interests are varied and diverse: she's passionate about women's rights, and is the Regional Head of her company's Women's Network. Since the pandemic, she's also been heavily involved in the wellness space, promoting mental health best practices and supporting colleagues with wellness content and activities. Neha is a voracious reader, insatiable traveller, fierce Krav Maga street fighter, and serial Mandala colourer. Her newfound hobbies include painting, running, long drives, and drooling over dogs and puppies. She is a practising Nichiren Buddhist who temporarily lives in Bangalore, India, and speaks English, French, Hindi, and Sindhi.

Follow her: https://www.linkedin.com/in/nehakirpalani/

Writing @typewritelove on Instagram